The Maze of Creation: An Alchemist's Guide to the Center

by Ricardo Tane Ward Ramirez

Little Crow Press

The Maze of Creation

The Maze of Creation:
An Alchemist's Guide to the Center

Copyright © 2019 Ricardo Tane Ward Ramirez

All Rights Reserved.

First Edition: August 2019

Without limiting the rights under copyright reserved above, no part of this publication may be reproduced, stored in or introduced into a retrieval system, or transmitted, in any form or by any means (electronic, mechanical, photocopying, recording or otherwise), without the prior written permission of both the copyright owner and the above publisher of the book. Please do not participate in or encourage piracy of copyrighted materials in violation of the author's rights. Purchase only authorized editions.

ISBN 978-0-9966299-2-8

Printed in the United States of America

Little Crow
Press

Austin, Texas

The Maze of Creation: An Alchemist's Guide to the Center

The Maze of Creation

~For Maria~

The Maze of Creation

Let me begin by reaching out on a human level, before we enter the Maze.

Thank you for reading. I'm sorry if anything I say here offends you. That is certainly not my intention.

I hope you enjoy the work. I wrote it just for you.

Much love to you and yours.

Peace

-RTWR

The Maze of Creation

Hatching means breaking every wall you've ever known.

The Maze of Creation

PROLOGUE

The Maze of Creation

Prologue

Life is a dream unfolding from a great unconsciousness. We try to make sense of formulas and symbols; we create sciences and religions, all while truth lies just beyond comprehension and transcendence lies in waking up. To truly awaken is to leave this world, to no longer be caught in a dream. This is the maze we are lost in.

If I may show you the way, please follow.

I can't tell you that you're lost. It's just something you feel; confusion is intuitive. A dim light illuminates notwithstanding. Shadows dance on cavern walls to a faint music, but perhaps we cannot make out the tune. Something is just out of reach. What is it that you seek? Happiness? Freedom? Knowledge? I cannot promise that you will find them, but looking is important.

The happy and free dance right through their lives. I commend them for this. However, often the firmly rooted become too stiff to sway with the wind, while the free may find the soil athirst. So often are the successful the least fulfilled while the wretched seem happiest. Who is really lost — the seeker or the ignorant?

Whether or why we are happy or successful can seem like the most important thing in life. Contentment leads to complacence and even comfort. But unease gnaws deeper and deeper into your soul. We are tense and need release. We are bound and need freedom. We are uneven.

Let's try to balance.

The Maze of Creation

Breathe in.

Breathe out.

Take in the toxic fumes that others emit and purify them into fragrance. Swallow their insults, their rejections and their misunderstandings — do not respond in kind. Give them light, love, and knowledge. When they reject it, give them more. They cannot throw it away forever.

Expect nothing of this world — reciprocity is your job. It is not random, nor ordered. Chaos lives but does not reign. Law is one. Balance. Try to hold on and it will whisk you away. Try to let go and it will crush you.

Wisps of clouds slowly usher eons of drunken lives lived just to piss and die to give back to a creator that asks nothing in return. Too many people are drawn by an apocalyptical passion to destroy this world. Masses look to snap away all humanity and to free the world from our virus.

And yet what of all that we made?

What of the pyramids, the temples, the songs and the dances — the designs in our lives that we created to honor the divine? What is it worth as the world burns beneath our feet? How can we so readily discard humanity, culture, and life as we know it — the world as we have made it?

Prologue

For centuries even war was beautiful, to say nothing of peace. Our kings were poets ordained to channel divinity and interpret divine law. Jeweled crowns of gold pulled knowledge into the Sahasrara chakra so that the anointed could speak the words of gods. Knowledge was anchored in gnostic prayer and earth ritual in order to create and sustain great societies.

Who taught you that everything that came before modernity was a lie? Who crippled the imagination of our children with lies of their own? The first thing kids learn in school is that there is no magic, there are no spirits and that the world is dead. They learn that the voices that they hear in the wind and the impulses to sing at random are distracting illusions to the important task of obeying orders from sad bureaucrats.

Mediocrity and competition weed out brilliance and foster obedient soldiers in the ongoing war against the divine law of creation. More and more dull and vile they have shaped us in their institutions and the science of monotonous pulling of levers on machines built for terracide. Those unwilling to flip their assigned switch are shown that they do not belong. Drugs and cages are administered to the slaves that run away.

Violence is the order where God has been killed. They wield his body on a stake. They celebrate their obedience on a flag. Those who do not salute mark an unruly light that is dampened through isolation, chemical addiction, a social pull towards self-destruction.

Even those who would claim to save the world are obsessed with its destruction. Warped senses of obligation repeat underlying lies of the father anti-culture. The indoctrinated part of us keeps us from envisioning the future we want.

Even when truth is, for a moment, seen and felt, it is rarely treated with reverence. Quickly it is wielded as a weapon to kill the immediate threat. Seldom is the sapling truth cultivated into a formidable tree that could provide the shelter we so desperately need. We are so hungry that we consume unripe fruit and shit seeds into sacred water that we flush into septic systems.

The internal obedience to the convenience of the slaughter of others and even ourselves, presumes that all hope is lost…

But it is not.

Prologue

The missing piece reveals a clue.

Change is slow,

But the grasshopper bounds forward in an instant.

A CAT

The Maze of Creation

A Cat

A cat, it so happened, was watching the entire time. Sometimes a scraggy tabby searching for scraps in an alley, sometimes a jaguar stalking the jungle — always a cat though and always watching. Within the labyrinth of dreams that we could not wake up from, he walked upon the walls looking down at the lost wanderers hitting dead end upon dead end. He wanted to help them reach the Center, to awaken from their nightmare — but how? He could not speak their language.

And so one day he decided to enter the Maze. He hopped down from a high wall, as cats do, and immediately began to transform into one of us. He became blind and weak; no longer possessing the agile superpowers of a cat. He found himself a man. And the labyrinth, once so clear a circle with a center and a definite direction to be followed, was like a world, wide open with rivers and mountains.

The cat was lost and he could feel the truth slipping from his mind. He had to speak it out. He found a Cyprus tree and whispered into the hole in its trunk all the secrets he possessed.

"Go and tell the others", he said.

And the tree obliged.

The Maze of Creation

The Cyprus encoded the truth of the cat in its leaves, branches and roots. The other trees learned to mimic this truth and pulled in the wind to sway them into a song. They danced a pattern of a circle within an endless set of circles with divinity in the middle. Thus did the cat create a place of truth for humans to find, a center where knowledge can be known. This maze became a map to the center of creation, a language to decipher this riddle, a truth that could be learned, an awakening.

This is the way through the Maze, as I have learned it. I invite you to heed the directions. They lead to the Center, where you have been headed all along.

ENTER

The Maze of Creation

Enter

The directions are simple enough: enter the labyrinth, cast out fear and doubt. Know that we will succeed here in this world and in this lifetime. Do not despair. You will reach the Center.

As you enter the Maze, it is dark. There is mystery, but you can uncover what is embedded within. The first wall is doubt.

Turn Left

Leave behind those who doubt you. Abandon the institutions they built. Everyone and everything that has denied you strength of ability or will is of no use to you here. The extractive impulses encoded into the social world that raised you will drain you. This begins with you doubting yourself — like they taught you to do. Do not doubt yourself. You will succeed.

The next wall is wanting.

Turn Right

Allow yourself love and happiness. Do not suffer here. It is easy to feel that you do not deserve to be happy and free with all the suffering in the world outside. Your happiness is your compass. In order for your judgment to be sure, it must be tuned to your emotions. Allow feelings to guide you. Learn to carry happiness and joy in your heart in any situation with anything you do. Hard as it may seem, this will help you see in the dark.

The Maze of Creation

The next wall is resentment for those who do not follow the path. They will try to stop you when they see that you are free and happy.

Turn left

Forgive them in your heart. Pray for them. Love them, even your enemies. To turn right at this wall is so often the misstep of the righteous soul who seeks justice in the Maze. It is a trap. The only justice is at the Center, and we still have a long way to go.

Remember, the only true political division is the side of compassion and forgiveness and the side of judgment. May all those on this side pray for those on the other — that they may join us.

The goal is for all of us to find enlightenment. Not just you.

Enter

When the Center was first created in this realm only one man knew of its existence – the cat. The trees all knew and spread the message to all plants, whom have kept this secret ever since. They humbly guard a million truths within their leaves and vines — a million keys to a million locks to the doors within our minds.

The birds too found the clearing from above. They entered and found the cat there all alone. They exchanged knowledge of the Center for knowledge of the world surrounding it. They too could see a maze with walls where languages miscommunicate and actions end in vain. They taught all language to the Center and gleaned the greater word from that center. They looked for those who could hear them. Those who understood bird language entered into the Maze. They too had a long way to go. You are not alone.

Find the world around you — a distraction of sights and sounds.

Turn Left

Honor with humility the knowledge of the plants and learn from them. This is a lifelong gift that will guide you to the Center.

Turn Left again and listen to the sounds of the birds. They can guide you to the Center, but you must learn to listen first. Do not get lost in thinking. Listen.

And when you can listen properly, you will learn also to be heard.

It is important to cultivate your own voice.

Learn to speak. Be careful and clear with your words. A paralyzed tongue is freedom surrendered.

If your word choice hinders communication, change it.

There is no need to be a prisoner to ideas of any kind.

Disposition is dynamic. Form should be as creative and diverse as possible. Mutes fear judgment. Chatterboxes are insecure. Poise in presentation is mere drapery for substance.

Truth simply is.

Find it.

Truth is found in the story of creation. In order to know the world, you must learn how it is made. Then shall you understand why we are all here.

CREATION

The Maze of Creation

Creation

Before form or shape, before light or sound or depth or breadth was swirling darkness — a primordial womb in which our universe gestates — timelessly eternal, formlessly expansive — infinity as zero — no thing... yet.

There, in that darkness did form take shape as a point, a center. Still to be divided into smaller pieces of a great circle, a radius formed. And from there a diameter halved totality and birthed a dual nature of light and dark, hot and cold, stillness and movement, growth and decline, life and death and all dual orders of the universe.

Creation as a divine principle is a source. All comes from the source, and in the end all returns. Every change we cannot trace in our world is a connection to source. All light emanates from the divine.

All remained equal parts except for the center, and thus it became the Center. There was born light as a unique and creative force — an intelligence looked out upon itself and saw that it was center and circle, and radius and whole halved. It saw that it was light and that it was darkness, good and evil, life and death, and the mere idea that these others could exist, brought them to be. So too did the reflection turn inwards as a conscious being who for the first time said,

"I exist.""

And from then on was there existence.

The Maze of Creation

From creation was there knowledge.

Knowledge is sacred. It is the foundation of all relationships — and the foundation of knowledge is divine. As language is too clumsy a tool to navigate such a truth, so do the dark passageways of the labyrinth lead many astray. In seeking to understand, the grasp suffocates the same flower emitting the life-giving scent.

Knowledge is a relationship to be cultivated. A series of relationships amongst all things — knowledge is the law that binds us together to something greater. Those who have glimpsed reality, who have entered the Center of the Maze, have found there the totality of the world — within all and all within.

CREATION

Turn Left

Care for others. Live in service to this world. There is nothing more fulfilling than tuning in to the reciprocal law of nature. The more you do for others, the more blessings will come to you.

The more selfless in your actions, the more you will feel connected to others.

Our natural impulse to care for others has been subjugated by a drive towards domination. Reject the impulse to conquer.

Instead find strength in service. There are always those lower in social rank. Work to dissolve the ranks as you extend yourself towards those in need.

Don't try to carry too much. You have only two hands. But let your vision become the container that allows you to carry in abundance. Focus on where and how you move. This will allow you to take forward what you need.

The Maze of Creation

Turn Right

Do not forget your freedom. Do not abandon your happiness and your pleasure.

Here too, many get trapped. We get stuck in giving too much to others and not enough to our selves. Take care of yourself first.

There are more lessons there in that mistake that illuminate the path beyond. There is still a long way to go.

Turn Left

Do good works. Service to others is essential to finding our way through the Maze. If and when you can help others is a gift to your higher self. The longing to love within your heart is fed by simple acts of kindness. When we struggle to give, we can always count on those in need to be there. Indeed they are plentiful.

Give to the needy, but do not carry their burden. To give pity to others adds weight to their circumstances. You lighten their load when you lift, and you lift with lightness. Joy and laughter carry more than commiseration.

CONFLICT

The Maze of Creation

Conflict

Conflict has always existed outside of the Center. Since the beginning has there been turns in the Maze, the missteps along the way: the evil, murder, rape and suffering that make man question the reality or validity of a god. They hit a wall and turn around.

Here you have must learn to scale upwards. The wall has a path of its own in your 3 dimensional maze. You tread along with new knowledge, asking not how but "why?"

Upon the crossroads of this world, the mystic walks the vertical road beyond that of human drama, while his sisters and brothers struggle along horizontal axis. You must know both as you venture further, upwards into the labyrinth.

Remember when we turned Left, away from judgment and blame of others? With faith in what is greater we turned our cheeks; we disregarded drama, and now we see the law we follow, that steers us away from our natural tendencies.

We had to ask "why?" at one moment or another. Why were we all made to suffer in this world? Why is there pain and war? And what can we do about it?

We cannot merely turn away like a hapless hermit and live amongst the wolves. There must be an answer and indeed there is.

The Maze of Creation

Turn Left

Know once again that the infinite holds all darkness and light. Know that pain is equal an instrument of the divine as joy. But remember too that goodness holds a small margin over evil. This is the Center that remains as light. This is the crown of God. It is the pure center and here is the circle whole. Here is the greater cycle complete.

The structure that shook the trees as this world was created was birthed long ago in the mind of the creator. Everything in this world has been made as a mirror of the cosmic mind of God. As creation begets creation, so too has this world been formed, and our souls, and our lives. This sacred knowledge comes to us, but with limitations.

Just as we put a name to God, so do we fall from our new path and back upon the road below. Corruption of all that is holy has its story too. This story we can learn and perhaps the best way is to fail.

Fail. It is only human to do so.

It's important to make mistakes, accept them and grow.

Fall — but get back up.

CONFLICT

God is infinite.

The totality of the universe is divine.

Goodness holds a small edge over evil.

This gap is the crown of God.

Within the whole both the good and the bad are God.

We may rest in darkness, but must not deny the light.

Accept evil as crucial to the whole.

Know that light maintains a margin over darkness.

Know the totality.

Know the infinite.

Know the divine.

BALANCE

The Maze of Creation

Balance

When the universe was still young, in the mind of the Creator, he began to explore his existence. He balanced the hot and the cold and the dark and the light. But he could not do so in stillness. Balance only came in surges of one energy pushing into the other and receding when the other pushed back in. Thus balance and movement were born together.

As substance began to appear in the creator's mind it reflected in the world he created around him. The more he would explore in his mind, the more complex would the shadow world become. Thus the mind and the world around remain connected through all creation. So too is the universe mediated in movement and balance.

Turn Left – Spin into movement

Turn Right – Maintain Balance

These tools will come into play as we proceed. As we move through the Maze, we will spin and balance as needed.

The Maze of Creation

As the world became more complex with form and sound vibration, Creator made lands and beasts and bodies. He experimented by giving drives of desire and fear to the beings he created. Soon the hot and cold took on new modes of movement of the shifting tides of chase and flee, grow and decline, appear and expire. With each new combination of forces interacting, a new aspect of knowledge was born. And so Creator became yet more expansive and the infinite reaches of a single swirl became a dense ecosystem of what would soon become stars.

Turn Left

Know that big things have small beginnings. Understand that time moves slowly but that it always moves. Find alignment with the rhythm around you and hold on.

Do not command the ocean. Ride the wave.

Balance

Everything that existed in the beginning was a thought in the mind of Creator. And as he realized this, he thought of thinking and created a new being that could think and thus create with its own mind.

So was born the riddle of where the Creator's reach extended.

Were the thoughts and creations of his thoughts and creations merely a continuation of his own self or were they new beings with agency of their own?

As the exponential creation of creators expanded throughout the universe, the infinite reached the limit of its own paradox — creation creating creation creating creation — all a single mind knowing itself and also a hive-mind of gods creating each other.

Gods interact through the movement and balance that holds them. Each deity creates new worlds or pieces of what become more intricate, complex and beautiful with every connection, realization, interplay or thought. It is within this ecosystem that our world was created as but a fleeting musing of a mind within a mind. For this reason our world works as a reflection, and as we will see, we are not so different from these early creators birthed at the dawn of time.

Turn Right

The Maze of Creation

This is the dawn of the future. There is something greater moving through you. This does not negate your agency — it is your agency.

Creation is an ongoing process. We are part of this process.

Creation is the thinking mind of which each of us is a synapse firing. Creation is God learning.

Our presence here on this planet is as important as anything in the universe. The way we think is key to how we act and live. Systems that are created conscious of the connection to creation, maintain balance. The dominant ethos in the world today does not honor our connection to creation and produces imbalance.

Turn Left

Be in creation

Create

Know that balance is the goal and beauty is the chariot that she rides in. Steer with beauty all you create to balance this world and honor creation.

BALANCE

God is not wise.

God is wisdom.

God will not save you.

God is salvation.

God did not create you.

God is creation.

Disembodied, she is a higher form of knowledge.

Our minor language, confined to limited dimensions,

Cannot even chart her waters.

OUR WORLD

The Maze of Creation

Our World

Before the Earth was created Father Sun put down tobacco, gave thanks and prayed.

Our world was created long ago — a manifestation of God formed in a new center. A primordial Sun stretched into the surrounding space, searching for something solid to make worlds. From chaos into order is a beautiful transformation: paint on canvas, spools of thread woven into patterns.

A raw spirit must be cultivated into elements. Fire always exists as the base of energy, but it can only direct back to source.

Father Sun was formed as a new center, as a collective of gods, as a singular ball of light. This formation was part of the birth process of our earth and solar system.

Turn inwards — you are but a spec.

Turn outwards — you are infinite.

Unfold the maze within you.

Where is your center?

How shall you find your way through creation as it unfolds, lest you be both creator and creation at once?

The Maze of Creation

The map of this world gives dimensions to our existence. That is why creation itself plays such an important role in how we understand the world.

Whatever you do, start by giving thanks — always.

This is the first ingredient of all creation — gratitude. To honor what has come before is to ensure that it remains in some form. Whether burned for fuel, mulched for soil, stripped for parts, or eaten as food, the pieces of the past are the means of the future.

Adorned as muses or whispered as warnings, all that has come before is teacher helper and friend.

Give thanks for every mistake. Give thanks for every fall, every fail, misstep, trip, stumble and stupidity. These teachers make us swift and surefooted to climb yet higher over new grounds. The trails ahead lead over the mountains and into the fertile valleys below. Thanks comes from the greater gift of the Earth and her abundance.

All we consume is thanks for who we are and what we bring. Give a pinch of tobacco to the Earth, as you are a pinch for her left here to bless the world around you.

Turn Right

Pray. Give thanks.

Our World

This world is a blessing, born in thanks. It is an honor given to God. The Earth is the very fruit of abundance, and fertile soil of souls that is cultivated by the gods.

The mother holds us all in her womb, impregnated by God, the light giving Sun. Such love that it transcends the physical has been given the name of God. For this reason the mother has been called the Virgin — impregnated by light, not by heat. Fruits of love and not desire she bears on her branches.

If only we could remain in the warm waters of the dark. But we are born as all things in this world in the wind of chaos. Our world is not born from a single source. Movement is unstable and with only Sun and Earth such complex creations as we now know would not be possible. The history of our world is of the evolution and growth of this place and of us within it.

The Moon anchors stability. Four fish swim at equal distance from the Center in a circle. A silver plate rests discarded amongst stones — the lid to a cosmic cooking pot.

Our world is a circle squared by a center with four posts. Our world is a finite reflection of what is infinite and holy. While the center of all things is made of light, the sides are made of solid, liquid, gas, and energy. These elements were the swirling beasts fished out by the silver of God.

The Maze of Creation

Deep in the primordial darkness, elements are dragons. The Sun baited himself to draw them in. When the beasts emerged from the depths for a bite he speared them. They flailed and thrashed about. A stalemate formed in the lock of battle until grandmother came back from the Center with a plea for peace.

Grandmother saw the struggle from her deep surroundings, and understood that the brutal violence taking place would crush the fledgling world if not tempered by love. She beseeched her son to be careful.

She said

"Do not destroy what you cannot control. Have no vanity. Give of yourself, so that others may be fulfilled."

And it was so that the god felt compassion for the beasts with whom he struggled, and he gave to them so that we all might live. He cut off his head as an anchor for the Earth. This light and darkness merged together and became the moon. The formation process began to vibrate into a musical rhythm. The beasts froze in hypnosis of the sphere.

The god then cut off his arms and legs and fed one each to the four elements. They filled with light. They too took shape as orbs and began to dance to the celestial tune. Father Sun remained as a heart to give center. He conducted his co-conspirators to weave together the world being born, and they complied.

Our World

Turn Left

Give sacrifice. It is the key to creation, stability and balance. Sacrifice holds the life giving power of the divine within its act. The outer planets were formed through struggle and sacrifice, and to this day they play a part in all human creation. They are the elements that sustain this world. They are the senses that allow us to get through the Maze. Each one gave a gift to create life on this planet: an ear, a nose, skin and eyes. These pieces allowed beings to form, and through many stages did life flourish based upon the four elements, and anchored by the cyclical dance of the Moon. New life rippling through a newborn world felt, heard, tasted and saw the fractured consciousness of demigods.

The Maze of Creation

Turn right

Use your senses. Trust your body as an extension of all other bodies: heavenly, earthly, elemental. Know your senses as but small parts of a greater whole that guide you, and the rest of us, through this maze.

Learn the gifts given to know and appreciate the beauty and splendor of the world. Protect the elements of creation that sustain us all. Not just dragons, not just elements, but also something more, something deep — the spirits that make our world.

Follow the planets in the sky. Speak to them and listen to what they say. Talk to the fire and the water; listen to the earth and the wind. Be in communion with creation through communication with nature. The rhythms of your heart — the intake of your senses are channels to the divine. Water is life so too are fire, earth and air. Behind the veil of space and time these dragons still swim in darkness, they too still circle the Sun as planets, give us life as elements, and sustain our animal form to experience it all.

STORY

The Maze of Creation

Story

As you get closer to the Center of the Maze, the purpose of everything becomes easier to see. Just as the language of the birds sounds more like words, so the meaning of each cloud and stone is animated. Animals and plants demonstrate that a greater movement is taking place through you all.

The path circles inward to a sharp spiral. Darkness dissipates as form is taken. Signposts point the way. This is the first you have been shown that you are moving in the right direction. You have found a pattern, but do not think that what you have learned is static.

Turn Right

All things grow, change and alter like the Moon. Study her. Pay attention to her cycles. Know that the structures in the labyrinth are of her design. A keeper of movement and a link to infinity resides within us all. The creation of our selves and our families takes precedence over our own selfish claims to this world.

The signs written on the face of the Moon — once-forgotten hieroglyphs speak clearly. You are divine. You must walk with this knowledge. This is a pace beyond — it has been shown to you.

Turn around and retrace your steps back through the spiral.

The Maze of Creation

Now with new eyes the walls have shifted. Dead ends are easy to spot. The possibilities however are only more abundant.

As you walk on you hear the story told as to why and how you move Right or Left, up, down into the dimensionally expanding crystal ship that carries you still further towards the Center.

Understanding often rests between science and mythology. A subtle puzzle pulls us towards a higher consciousness.

The truest form of knowing is the myth, taking place as a story across the sky, in our human world, and in our personal lives.

Archetypes mirror gods and their chaotic desires. Lessons learned play out again and again as guideposts to the path. Spherical cairns mark the cosmic road in the cycles spiraling towards the Center.

The Maze is a set of stories, a social world of gods and demigods, which takes place in a time between the formation of the Earth and our own time of human history.

The "in between" is always present. It is the skeletal frame for the flesh of our social world. Each unique aspect of our history, every twist or turn in our personal lives is written in the stars by a bygone bard still singing in echoes of light and darkness.

Story

Turn Left

Learn to know stories. Allow them space to nurture your dreams. Turn inwards yet again and see that you are the Maze that you tread. Each turn another lesson, another unfolding of your heart, arms and legs. Each loss and gain is another step in a cosmic dance. Every cry and laughter are words sang by gods. Each life and death are grains of sand in a painting that tell tales so much greater than we, and yet impossible without us.

How many steps have walked this maze before us? Incarnations of people have taken many forms. Although there seemed to be so many stories, in reality there are but a few. My story is yours. Yours is mine. Perhaps the mix of characters takes turns slightly differently in order or intention, but the story is written before it is spoken, and the ingredients are scant.

The Maze of Creation

Four elements of creation multiply amongst them seeking balance of hot and cold: the intuitive fire knows; the material earth is silent; the life carrying water wants; and the moving air thinks.

The balance of these ways of knowing our earth is anchored as a center of its own.

This is your life. Each element within you can be balanced.

Often we feed only the mind and ignore the heart. Often we neglect our bodies, microcosms of the Maze that move and shift in and out of balance. Learn from your bodies and teach them too. Train your intuition, your mind and your heart. Learn to learn and learn to balance.

CHANGE

The Maze of Creation

Change

Deep within the Earth, her mind reaches outwards to the stars beyond the darkness. She thinks us into being — an ever-evolving and infinitely diverse manifestation of heaven and earth take place as mountains and rivers, deserts and oceans, forests and plains. An ever-evolving series of ideas are held by the Mother in thought, sustained by the four elements in form, given life by the Sun, and changing with the gadget accuracy of the Moon.

The forms that take place in this world join the endless parade of creators that came before them, living beauty and pain, rising and falling again and again. This is your family. Everything in this world is a relative of everything else. We are mutually dependent on all others to live, to know, to love, to move, to understand, to be.

Step outwards into the world. Knowledge is a relationship. All we are given is antennae. Tune in to the divine voice of creation. Pick up the vibration of the song. Listen, not just to hear, but so you may sing.

The fertile earth was born as a virgin mother, able to hold life — an open book to be written. From across the cosmos, the stars, creators who had worlds of their own, sent down sacred seeds. Divine beings, with conscious desires and thoughts of their own, could now be born in new and exciting forms. Lands, beasts and flora emerged from the consummation of light sown down and the tilled rows of earth.

The Maze of Creation

Seeds were sent in light and received by the Earth who had to measure the dictates of time and space, energy and change and allow these worlds to emerge as collaborations of greater forces.

Seeking precedent and splendor upon abundance, the Earth and Sun did right by allowing the strangest creatures home here. Beauty was made over and over again as plants and grasses, birds and beasts, winds and clouds. Eons of creation passed before our time.

Turn Right

Know that this all happened before, in one way or another. Human drama was once merely the drama of the gods. The tales of the animals and demigods in all the various cultures of the world are true. They take place in the time of great truth and formation and for that reason sound similar to one another. Before humans formed, time moved differently and the makeup of this world was distinct.

CHANGE

In our version of time, there are epochs in the pre-world when we did not exist. Major changes took place in this distant timelessness. The foundation for the Maze preceded both time and humanity.

The old system of hunting the sacrifice had yielded a brutal and competitive order. Honoring the sacrifice of life-giving meat led to bloodlust for death. Competition gave way to battle. Men served their inner desires as extensions of hungry gods playing games with their souls. Rebirth gave way to too much forgetting. The old way looked holy no more.

The very map that we use to decipher twists and turns are the movements of the children of the old gods. These lesser planetary deities are closer still to us than their parents. They were born between epochs in order to add layers and complexity to the world. These gods were born just like us as agents of greater creation. So too are they a part of us, as they stir us into awakening

As keeper of time Saturn spat out Pluto, a rim to limit the reach of this world. So density and darkness ever pull downwards unto power through struggle. Uranus took out his anger by creating the bullheaded Mars, the harness of power within conflict. Neptune entreated Mercury to dance out knowledge directly from the Sun, so that we would know his music as the foundation of human culture and thought. And Jupiter, King of them all, passed his reign on to his own son — who was born to give us consciousness.

The Maze of Creation

The new light shot out from his father's heart, leaving the exit wound that became an all seeing eye. The father could rest now. His time as ruler came to an end. After searching for so long in the recesses of his own darkness did he find the forgiving heart within. It was this that came out from the source; a serpent danced right out of the Center and traced a spiral in the sky. Within us the strands of receptors, keepers of our serpent knowledge, were animated with his light. The morning was crowned with the new star and a new cycle was born.

The math amongst the Moon and Venus multiplied a series of potential equations and existing ecosystems of celestial spirits filled their variables into place. Thus was the shell awakened in new holy form. A mirror of the universe was the complete solar system, and now within like a jewel were born bodies finally free enough to house the souls of distant stars.

Venus is the animator of our will and his unique story has been told a thousand times. This is the story of the rise of human consciousness. It is born in myths all over the world. It is also true, every word.

Change

When the world was ready and the solar system finally formed, gods stormed the vessel to be created in this way, to know beauty and pain, to know consciousness, to be complete. The world they came to inhabit overwhelmed them. It overwhelms us still to this day.

The passion of life — the delight of knowledge — the power of creation — is it good or evil to know this much?

Stop. Calm down. Take a breath. See the light at the Center of the Maze — so close now. It emanates from your heart, not your brain. Thinking now will keep you from reaching the Center. Fear now will blind you.

Remember to remember.

Remember to love.

Remember that you already know.

You've been here the whole time.

MEMORY

The Maze of Creation

Memory

I know you recognize the story now — you have heard it a thousand times. I know your story too, because it is mine — one and the same. Perhaps variation of times and places have offered the illusion of exception. Beneath names are archetypes and around souls are things. Our stories are the baskets we weave to carry the world forward. You're in mine, and I yours. We dream each other into place with each stitch point.

Every thought we have brings human light into the prism of our macro-reality. Another layer of existence sediments historical silt from the Milky Way. The great river washes us downstream to awaken here and now, realizing that we have been traveling without the use of limbs or even consciousness.

Here, we are born. We are the very river, the water washing down. We are the light lowering from heaven. We are the very cycle of creation told in another form, hence not seen by God before now. Our story is our stories, our lives.

The great story of God and all of creation is the personal trials you have lived in your life. The battle of good and evil is your very soul. Consciousness is your very mind. The Earth is your very body, and mine.

This story is ours. We too are creators, gods in human form. Lest we forget our own stories and know that this is true.

Turn left into remembering.

The Maze of Creation

Memory is the basket's shape. Remember who you are, why you are here. Tell the story to remind others of their stories and why they, we all, are here; because we are here for a reason that we've forgotten.

Turn Left

Remember

The rise to consciousness is a long road of remembering. Deep in the slumber of solitude we are mindless; within the heart of God we are all-knowing. Here, we rest between, in the process of awakening that all things experience as they are brought into creation.

At first we see something curious within us and the mirror reflection of this quality elsewhere in the world. Synchronicity is a road trodden by co-creators of the universe. Remember we are the legs that walk this road.

When the Moon is full at its rise does he see his reflection in the setting Sun. The mimicking beasts in camouflage see their own environment: a toad, a stone; a moth, tree bark; a hare, the surrounding snow. The mirror shows the movement of our dances in the existing patterns of life: the shell of the snail in the unfurling frond of the fern is the galaxies and growing embryos around them.

Memory

All life is remembering that it belongs here. You should try not to forget that you belong here too. The mathematics and breathing techniques developed by ancients are maps of this road to consciousness. Plant medicines make good vehicles for travel. As we move, we understand that the way through the Maze is our shared story of remembering. To remember little things that once seemed insignificant is to cut stones for the construction of the road to illumination.

The cries and screams of children are those of beasts who came before us. The tears we shed are the very sea that warmed us to life. Our forms as limbs and backs mimic those of our monkey cousins; and we look back to see that perhaps we were once like them. But something happened...

Turn Right

Remember what happened to us, so that we could awaken.

Turn along that wall that leads you now ever closer to the Center of the Maze.

THE CENTER

The Maze of Creation

The Center

In order to know this world — the reflection of himself — God, the creators' creator, came here as a person. He is within all of us. He is just a little more good than evil. He is conscious. Each of us is this child of God. The knowledge of this truth has been called Krishna; it has been called Christ; it has been called Buddha.

This truth has guided men and women to love each other and to know they are all divine, as they are all love itself. So too has this truth been stolen and brandished as a weapon of our own demise.

God is creation. The world is a Quaternary — a cross. We ascend towards the high point, towards knowledge, towards the divine, by lifting the axis upwards. You have seen this cosmogram as the cross that is worshiped. You have seen there too the withered and suffering king who wears the heart-stitching of serpents on his head. This figure hangs dead, as when we die, we return once again to source. When we suffer, we know that the truth is within the suffering.

God is to know this world — to know that everything in this world is as fleeting as dust. To know this world is to suffer. To know this world is to love. To know this world is to be divine — like God.

Turn in to the Center.

Enter the circle.

Know this world.

Be divine.

The Maze of Creation

Are you lost? Have you found confusion yet? Can you find what is itself unknown?

Let go. Fall into meaning. Your own life is the path — your experience the map.

Now the Center is your own heart. Your own self is the very God you rejected. You thought that you were so clever for so long and in the end you realize it was you who was stumbling in the dark, struggling to be loved and understood — just like the rest of us.

To be found is to find. To teach is to learn. To connect with others is to know your self. It is the self that searches and seeks to be found. Divinity remembers itself through your awakening.

In the center of the labyrinth is a Minotaur — a beast of earth and perversion, much like you. Waxwings can take you away, but they will not help you to slay the beast. How then will you overcome this monster?

Reach deep within.

Remember.

The Center

Can it be the same forlorn Christ in the Center, this bullheaded thing? When you hold the mirror up in the Center of the Maze, does it show you the face of God as an unfurling lotus of infinite splendor, or does mystery lurk beneath the full beauty as a dark star still waiting to emerge?

The beast has suffered in his between state; and yet he has been at the Center this whole time — like you have been. He is possessed by confusion, expressed as an uncontrollable rage. The helpless, naked, bleeding higher self, mirrors the lower self, chained by his passions.

Will you meet the struggle with the same brute strength you have hidden in your belt? Will you summon the forces of chaos to do your bidding and decapitate that disgusting beast?

Or perhaps you will offer gratitude — a pinch of tobacco? Perhaps offer your own head as you embrace the bull crowned with crescent moon. Perhaps you will sacrifice yourself in love for this poor creature within you, ruled by his head. Perhaps you will love him with enough compassion that he does the same.

He kneels before you and offers his head. A new moon rises full of possibilities for change. The corpse of the man takes a new form. A cat appears to lead you back home.

RETURN

The Maze of Creation

Return

A cat — scruffy tabby from the alley — great tiger stalking the jungle — emerges from the place of sacrifice as a strong animal willing to take what it needs and to sit as a ruler over his own domain. The knowledge to navigate with certainty is a quiet power, a faithful dominance, a subdued ferocity.

But does this cat show how you will live in the world outside? How will you find your way back out of the Maze?

How would you get home?

The world is so broken, so lost and drawn towards its lowest forms and by its darkest fears. Every truth in creation has been perverted and brought into falsehood. Everything beautiful and good has turned ugly. How can we reveal the face of God to a world that has only ever known the concept as its own perversion?

The inverse of divinity cannot present itself as the wretch that it is, so it appears as precisely its opposite. Wickedness was also born in the primordial struggle. This world allows form to everything, the good and the bad equally. Lies were born. Hatred was born. Each of these has its place in creation.

How can we cure a wound while wounding with our insistence on taking without reciprocating? Even the knowledge that moves freely within us is unpaid for. What will you offer for this knowledge right here, right now?

You are the iconoclast ripping down your own god-self from

its understanding. You nail your own Christ-self to the cross. You slay your own Minotaur with anger. You wrestle with the elements that struggle around you.

In life and breath you bring pain and death — in the unintended consequences of poor choices or in the already laid out cookie cutter culture that spins the rules around you. We consume dishes of food and drink unpaid for: spoiled air, black smoke, and sickness. Why have we done this?

How quickly do we all become the hypocrite of our own teaching? You beat yourself down in struggle. Your compassion seldom turns inwards. A liar and a thief - a murderer and pillager are within your own mind. A thousand times have you been wicked, and still you cling to the shame of your actions.

A victim too have you been. The very raped and maimed by your hand is your own destitute corpse awaiting the proper rites and burial. Quenching dirt may lay your soul to suffer no more.

Part of you just wishes to die to rid the world of all this pain. To turn off this suffering, would you quiet your own song. To scream would you mute the song of God.

What does the reach of your depth uncover? A part of God was unwilling to sacrifice and became sickness. The unpaid debt of all that is taken without divine reflection stagnates as a plague.

Return

The greater work of the alchemist is to cure the sickness that is at the root of all ill. This is the way back out.

Forgive others. Forgive yourself.

You did not create any of this. Remember that death and suffering were created long ago — so too were lies and cheating.

When you take on these sins as your own invention you deny yourself as an extension of creation. Your mistakes are your teachers. These are your guides that shine light in the dark maze. When you reject, in shame, the flawed being you are, so too do you deny the divine within you. You deny the ever-evolving creation of this world that you administer. You deny being human.

Be human. That is your only job here. Make mistakes.

Learn.

Love.

Forgive.

Show gratitude.

Create beauty.

HUMANITY

The Maze of Creation

Humanity

We are all just humans trying to be loved, trying to be understood, struggling to belong to something and to find meaning and usefulness — trying and failing.

To struggle to connect is so human. It is rare to jibe with the universe with ease. The rhythms in our hearts seek beats of kindred souls. Interpreters of deep language find voice in creation, in love and understanding each other, in giving meaning and finding usefulness for one another.

How we stumble over our own confusion and the missteps of those around us. Self-loathing expresses a projection onto others.

Insecurity makes others insecure. Cries for help, harm. Attempts to sing, silences others. The shy and unsure are seen as aloof and judgmental. Rejection spreads in a ripple of mutual self-doubt.

Only when the self is loved by the self can we be understood. Only when we listen can we truly find our voice. It is spoken by our siblings, those who are not just like us, but who are us.

Oneness struggles to find itself over and again and instead finds a broken scattering of egos waiting to coalesce into a gold seal of light. Divinity struggles to give us meaning and we struggle to give meaning to the divine. But it is one and the same.

The Maze of Creation

Each and every person you see is divine; each one God.

Everything you see and touch in this world is here for divine purpose.

When we treat others as divine it is hard to judge them. It is easy to have compassion for the troubles of the world. When we see a disassociated individual, we often objectify them for our own purpose. While we might admire the divine beauty of a potential mate, we are unlikely to leer crudely at the same person when we see them as divine. While we might enjoy competition with a divine mind or body in order to train ourselves, we are less likely to feel wounded when we lose, once we understand that we are all the same. When we are at odds with others in political matters, we can see the troubles that consume them without moving to hatred, when we understand that we are embedded within the same errors.

Humanity

Actions are identity only when you don't know who you are:

Guilt becomes shame.

Regret makes you a ghost.

Longing binds legs. Greed blinds eyes.

Envy empties pockets.

To know who you are guides behavior:

Pride becomes honor.

Redemption gives life.

Presence is freedom.

Humility opens perspective.

Generosity creates wealth.

"But who am I? — You ask.

Your heart knows the answer.

You are human.

The Maze of Creation

The depths of the world are profound in simplicity. Ceremony rounds errant impulses into circles. Spirals spin together scattered stories. The many are one and the ones are many, moving back-and-forth in various pitches and frequencies.

It is when the pitch is off when the mind freezes. Thoughts entangle in trap-laid hooks of social complexity. Clear paths close into dense underbrush. Our frequency of intent finds an equally tuned counter-intention. The distorted hum drowns out all other sounds. Now we are driven by the noise of conflict. We turn up the volume when we should tune up the frequency. We get stuck in stupid arguments designed to set us back.

Who controls the dial to your heart? Who sets the pace of your wanderings, or for that matter the destination? All paths lead slowly to the Center, whether we are caught in loops or break walls.

When we take aim at our prey, we cannot too slap the mosquito at our ankle. The rise to enlightenment and descent into power drown each other out. Can stillness illuminate your path? Can forgetting who you are show your true face and feelings?

Humanity

Even those with the same goals often fight their mutual stubbornness upon the other's tender heart. Often good intentions turn into sad supplications. Un-watered trees produce poor fruit. Out-of-tune guitars sound awful. Hearts out of balance miss the complimentary notes. We must all love and support each other. Even our enemies are our allies when we find the songs of the spiral. Tensions vibrate into new music. We reach high ceremonial peaks.

When we assert our strength we will always find resistance. But if we choose not to engage at the level of the tension and instead tune upwards through responding with love and empathy, then can we truly change this world.

As for the enemies you have collected, as individuals and families and groups, love each and every one. These poor souls struggling to be loved and understood for some reason find solace and strength in our misfortune. How lost must they be. And yet without forgiveness of their erroneous thoughts and actions, how could any of us have the strength to overcome our own self-doubt and inner rejection?

In your struggle you have hated them too and this has weakened you. When you realize you need strength, go to them with love. Do not let your own love and forgiveness be muted by servitude to others unwilling to grow. Begin in that small circle around you by first loving yourself, forgiving your family, those closest who have done wrong to you. Surely there you will find the strength to forgive and to love even the worst of monsters. From within does our sick society begin to heal.

Understand the tyrant who oppresses is within you. Forgive him. The sellout, the backstabber, the cheat and the snitch that you feel so nobly above, exist within you. If we combed carefully through your life's actions we would surely find — especially if we cast all excuses aside — the very traitor to our cause in you: the hypocrites lips on your face, the unfaithful countenance, the lust driven loins trace your shape in the sand.

Learn to forgive and in so doing learn to overcome. Do not judge others for their wrongdoings. To do so only shows insecurity for your own failings. Once you recognize that you are pointing in the mirror, you can accept who you are, and leave the tension behind. There will be no need to speak ill of others again. There is no need to drag yourself back the way you came. Now you will lift others up. Forgive them. Teach them. Learn from them.

Build relationships with this world. This is the map leading back home.

Humanity

Compassion is measured amongst enemies, not allies. To hold those who scorn you is unlike holding a friend.

Your innermost anxiety is a refusal to embrace who you really are.

The shame that cripples your esteem steers your empathy for others. Let go of the reins. Fall into peace.

When credit is due, step back.

When responsibility beckons, step forward.

It is only with purpose that you shall exit this Center.

Only after the purge can you take in air again. After you have vomited every drop of self-hatred are you permitted to move.

The first step back is to forgive once again. This time forgive yourself. Forgive yourself for every step out of line, every mistake. Each teacher that showed you the truth must be honored. And now the honor extends to all people — mirrors of God, good and evil. So you accept your self as you accept everything else that exists in this world.

The way back is learning too. It is a way of being and a way of teaching. It is a responsibility — take it!

POWER

The Maze of Creation

Power

Chaos did its bidding in the newly formed world. It does so still. Moving away from the Center disperses unity into a variety of forms, consistently pulling apart and crashing together in violation of the space and sovereignty of their neighbors.

The burbling beginnings began to battle as their fathers had before in aeons embedded in the sky above. Form struggled across stretches of too many and too few — a boundless sprawl rippled throughout matter and spirit until it hit a wall and bounced back. The wall — just another wave of power — was too sent shooting back way it came until meeting another. Soon, power began to find silence.

Thus was born the boundary, sleek and quiet and yet still all-seeing. He pained eyes upon his body as the watchman, keeper of the peace and guardian of the night. He became sovereign. He became jaguar.

The jaguar is a channel of the divine — matter as energy — transformation of light into shadow — through the creation of form, of balance, of law. He is the socket directly receiving the power of light. In this way, he is darkness — the container.

Nature does not judge. She just gives of her plentiful bounty. So shall you give as does mother, asking nothing in return. So the wellspring of love in your heart always shines on all things as payment. Lift only upwards and hear the psalms of praise in birdsong and tree shade.

The animals will show you the way. The lessons they lead are good examples of what to do and how to be. Give them the respect they deserve. Show them you are listening. In time you will learn that they are listening to you as well. You will see that all of your actions are reflected by them. Your good example will be received with harmony in the world reflected back to you.

How we understand power is important for our lives. To hold power is to refract light. To channel the divine light into strength creates mastery. In nature everything is eaten by another. The jaguar is king. He exacts tribute from the forest. In our world, the king is the jaguar — exacting tribute — embodying power in human form.

Power in society is war, exploitation and domination. There is an extractive element to power and a potency. Power is the electricity running our cities, our phones and our computers. Power is agency; it is knowledge incarnate as technology and force.

Power is dark. To gain something in this world is to pull it from somewhere else. We conquer in our small pleasures and minor acts of domination. Culture is woven together as a dense ecology. Here you are made from darkness and infused with light.

Power

A vessel fills with life-giving waters, so too does matter fill with energy — this is power — the gentle alchemy animating life. This is the embodiment of agency as a spiritual principle.

Our kings once sat on jaguar thrones, exacting tribute from their subjects. So too shall you receive tribute from the world around you — the millions of tiny prayers woven into the patterns that pull you through life. Breathe in these offerings that line your blessed life. Exhale them from your unclenched jaw with the calm countenance of a tiger. Learn how to receive. Learn to exact darkness from the lower world.

The Maze of Creation

The Jaguar does not control the forest.

But he is a master there.

He rests in the greater power.

So shall you rest in a greater power.

And may be a master here.

Only a fool tries to control the world.

COMPASSION

The Maze of Creation

Compassion

Do not grieve for the fallen, or feel shame for the sick. Give light to that darkness with a laugh. You were here too not so long ago. Help them up. All others can and will reach the Center too. There is abundant life for all.

Those who are stingy with knowledge are stingy with love. They give little because they have little to give. Do not pity such lost children. Do not judge the chick before it has left its nest. The flight you will show them in your grace and sweetness will give them the courage to soar yet higher than you ever dreamed.

It is so important that we forgive, and so important that we know the truth about God and creation, because what has been done to the Earth is so foul. The root sin is the very subjugation of God and creation by the hubris hands of man. As we all well know — ruin reins supreme.

However, do not be afraid. This Maze is a key that opens many doors. This is a bridge to cross the torrent that is the cruel and mundane quotidian existence.

Every step you take, from now on, is blessed. Every person you meet will be an angel in disguise. Remove the bandages from your eyes. You will find many layers of grot clouding what you assumed were clear panes of sight.

The Maze of Creation

How would you look upon the past? Your old self, so fearful and yet comfortable in his cower, beckons you to go back the way you came in. Another part of you will remain in confusion, and wish to stay in the Center.

Locking the doors to the church and boarding up the windows keeps the vampires out — yes. But your calling is to slay them in the streets. Walk with the cross and the stake. Know evil and corruption. This is part of the world too. God is evil. God is corrupt. How could it be otherwise? God is everything!

Compassion

Strength is delicate

Strength is gentle

Control yourself

Lest you be controlled

To control others breeds weakness

Care for them

Take responsibility

Wield strength

Accept that this world is ugly. Know ugliness, so that you may know beauty. Know pain so that you can feel comfort. Embrace hate, that you may give love. Accept death so that you may acquire life.

There has always been and will be evil and suffering in this world. Our job is to soothe and heal — to be heat for the cold. Do not deny the darkness — illuminate it. As for your own self, can you nearly eliminate evil — but only so much as you can tether to an anchor for the steady pull of your goodness. Assuredly the good within you would be meaningless without the evil against which it vies for air.

Hatred is heavy and stirs our worst nature. Evil is powerful; so powerful in fact that in its service one can amass basically anything: power, pleasure, riches. But you can never achieve love through hatred, because love is more powerful. Hatred cannot bring about compassion and forgiveness.

Compassion is active work. It is striving to listen and to constantly learn. Too much self-focus can blind us to the importance of cultivating enough humility to let go of our emotional attachment to anger. We inherit generations of trauma and feel it is our duty to bring voice to our own indignation. We want to shine a light on abuse and bring justice into the world. When we fail to do so repeatedly it is painful. This is where a forgiving heart will take care of you. It will pull you towards the greater justice. This too is where hatred will destroy you. Negative attracts negative. We get stuck in the mud.

Compassion

Within the light-filled Center it is nearly impossible to find the shaded door leading back into the world.

The alchemist finds gold in excrement. Do not be afraid of filth. Compost it into soil. Do not fear fire — allow it the air it needs to cleanse the ground. Do not fear the beast within you. Face the evil where it lies. Humility accepts vice — everything in moderation (including sometimes moderation).

The god in your own heart is corruption. The lie is on your lips. Here you will find the power to overcome deceit. Here will you find the truth. Power walks softly — each step a blessing, every glance a radiant light.

Step now out of the Center, and back into the Maze.

Maze walls are dark city streets. The black dog bites your thigh. Your friend fails to connect with you. You're late for something. You are the bearer of bad news. You broke another heart. The obsidian weighs you down and the lake is deeper than it has ever been. The world is still here and still cruel and hard. Even though you have an answer, most will not be able to hear it.

THE FIELD

The Maze of Creation

The Field

The Maze is now a field to cultivate. Plant seeds and nourish them. This is life-long work. Think now in terms of hundreds, even thousands, of years. Ensure the survival of this world. This means going slowly.

Do not get in front of yourself. To do so, is to get in front of the divine, and this is how evil sets in. This happens in the mythological time too. As the unnamable becomes named, so too does the relative become object, even the human becomes a body. The growth and dynamism of the world become stale. Beauty hardens. This is the world of "facts", a false sense of security, charting data regarding the plasticity of the mortar of the Maze's walls.

The answers you now seek are rooted in a different form of knowledge; not a collection of assorted ideas, but a series of relationships — all conscious and all connected.

Instead of seeking freedom by smashing the walls with hammers in vain, you add new bricks and mortar. Instead of mastery over, you now seek mutual respect. The inner Maze reflects a calm completion of the design around you.

Turn outwards — help your people through leading by example.

Honor truth — nurture it.

Honor knowledge — plant it.

Honor love — reap it from this world — not in struggle, but in peace.

Tune upwards.

Extend the wavelength

Slow down

Relax

The Field

To worry about ego is ego

Just be cool

The Maze of Creation

Walk back from the Center. Take care of what you have learned. Treat everyone as a god, with respect and reverence.

Know that creation is ongoing, and that change is always present.

Use the four elements of creation within you. Honor them. Balance them in your self, in your life: to think, to love, to feel, to understand. Apply this to the responsibility you have assumed. Care for your body, your family, your home, your work, friends, your community, the plants, and the animals, even the Sun, the Moon and the stars — love them all.

Take responsibility for healing yourself. Extend this healing outwards to touch all of your relations. With humility, without judgment, with the divine in your heart, walk into the world and create, love, be.

Turn right

Feel Joy. Feel sorrow. Through all the pain, do not forget to laugh. Remember not to fret. This is merely part of the path, not a wrong direction.

The Field

How will you now keep the Maze moving? How would you keep God from being named? How will you keep the knowledge sacred, and the soul from corrupting?

The straight line of truth offered in the fact-driven Science of the modern order is blinding in vision. In order to hold the truth, you must construct a maze.

Within riddle has the mystic hidden truths; in parable does read the holy scripture.

Take care to guard what you have learned within your practice and not in your mouth. The preacher leads sheep to the nourishment of their unthinking law. The flock recreates the pen again and forever. The monk allows the seeds of truth to mold and rot in his locked temple shed. The maze-keeper shall find a game, a coyote dance, a joke and put the truth inside.

We all change and this world wants us to succeed. We will win in the end.

Engage with the world.

Turn Right

Have fun.

Play.

THE SPIDER

The Maze of Creation

The Spider

The spider weaves a map of the universe. So tenderly does she emit a simulacrum of the movement and pattern of space — all to sustain her — to kill her prey in this world. A tiny tiger is queen of the cupboard jungle. But in the world beyond she sits at the center of time — before anything begins and after it's all over.

Everything is equal-distant to the Center. We are a perfect orb. The crossroads are divine places where sticky strands that trap the witless meet the road that the huntress stalks. Crosshatching the world below of work and soil, and the one above of prayer and stars.

Everything is within the Maze. The priest is a predator, keeper of the crossroads — keeper of knowledge. Where is the fly you will catch in your web? Without intention you will catch what you cannot eat or perhaps nothing at all. Without differentiating between the types of web, you will get caught yourself in the painful lessons of your scripture.

Accept your fate as a prosperous being and create an intention for achieving your goals. Accept your place in the world as a creator of the universe, as the setter of traps, a taker of life and the weaver of webs.

The Maze of Creation

We are all embedded in a larger web. We are all prey and predator. We are all tiny compared to something else and to others we are terrifying. Walk in a pattern, learn your place, fulfill your duty, and make hard choices. Keep space clean and time orderly. Create from within you. You have the means to weave the web.

The life that you live is a tapestry of infinite complexity. The threads are your consequences and too often they tangle in knots.

Learn to go slowly. Learn to weave on a single loom. Dedicate yourself to a craft; this will be your instrument for weaving. Too many mediums are unmanageable. Too many unfinished products produce stress. Learn to focus — the balance of mind and heart and hands will bring out the design.

LOVE

The Maze of Creation

Love

We struggle to live, find shelter and nourishment — all of us — to find love. So why not love each other? Why not nourish each and every one with the strength of your love? Why do we not shelter and feed each and every person in need? We have the means.

Are we such fools that we deny our own hearts love? Deny our own society peace? Deny our own species unity? Deny our own world life?

We have the strength in our love to be heard and to unite people for peace and healing. We struggle, each of us in our hearts, and therein shall we find the strength.

You fantasize about being free somewhere, out there in the wind. But you are your own jailer. Your own insecurities are the bars of your prison. Accept yourself — let yourself be loved. Let yourself be free. No one is your master. No one is anyone's master.

Each and every one of you is free. Even those of you kept in cages. Stand up and dance — claim your liberation. Move and express the greater voice within all things.

Beauty and love exist within you and for you. Be happy and free. Receive this love from yourself. Give thanks to yourself and for your self, your life, and your freedom.

Dance.

Give all that you have to joy. Feed happiness through movement and song. Dance away sadness and sing away grief. Use the tools of beauty to alleviate your pain and that of the world.

Are we such fools as to allow the world to be ruled by the worst of us — and by the worst in us? Our anger and fear has too often taken precedence over our compassion and temperance. So too have the most lost amongst us, in their blindness of conscience, elected themselves as the decision-makers and masters of the humble and hard working.

How shall we be ruled by the love in our hearts? Take responsibility to be ruled by the compassion this world gives you, so that you may accept yourself as the beautiful soul you are.

May that strength make you a leader in life — in your home, community, pueblo, and society.

May we guide the lost ones back to the compass of their own hearts, so that they may heal and rest and no longer burden the rest of us with their selfish and foolish misrule.

We are all in the process of creating the world around us. This is how culture is made. We create the political movement of our societies in our minor acts and in our civic engagement. The path to healing this world does indeed lie in taking responsibility.

Love

What does it mean to perform alchemy?

Turning darkness into light — yes; but what about light into darkness, animating stillness to move, calming movement to be still? Disruption of old orders arms the stubborn beachhead against crashing waves.

Does Dionysus meet a threshold that heeds him to circle back again? Does Apollo throw off convention if so stirred by anomaly?

Does breaking rules demonstrate their necessity, like the coyote's hunger and raven's lust? Does the alchemist find the edges of tradition? Is the key the narrative within contradiction that would otherwise be trite aphorism if anchored in law?

How much light is there in the dark? How much more can we see if we close our eyes tight enough? I tell you the darkness is near endless but at its core is an illuminated beauty, a song sung by her very mother. The twists up inside her void will bring us ever colder to a frozen pit within. Death is prepared for by loving life. Meaning is met by enjoyment.

Let love be your vice. Do not stop it within you. Return again and again to the heroine in her eyes and the laughter cast in those memories. Do not shake the sweats she invokes for the heating of your heart.

Flow with the movement. Do not escape it.

The Maze of Creation

Speak truth

Stop being afraid to hurt them

They are already hurt

By lifetimes of accumulated trauma

To share your pain

Will bring healing

Heal

Then, shall you heal them.

Love

The Center of the Maze is your heart. This is your divine connection to source. This is your power to forgive, to create beauty and to know. This is the field to sow and the force to flex. Exercise the divine within you — act in love.

Love all things as an extension of the divinity that moves through you. Your agency and your divinity are one — God compels you to live as you breathe and to love as you heal. Do not deny yourself the peace that lies within you. Radiate a beacon to light the path for others. Never shine it in their eyes. Carry the Center forward.

Love.

EPILOGUE

The Maze of Creation

Epilogue

"How do you know?" she keeps asking. *Looking for knowledge still embedded in material evidence. Though you see the path as clearly as stone, your certainty will not convince her.*

He asks for proof. Thousands of years of millions of people over hundreds of cultures agreeing, and sharing the same experiences will not convince him. He is blinded by pride. Thus has the modern man been cultivated, to reject truth, advocate for the devil, to never rest, but endlessly struggle against the world.

Often, if an equation works, it becomes accepted. Objectivity enters upon independent confirmation of the stated principle. This does not work here. The movement of all things in relation to all things now sways us. When we sustain relationships with the natural world, there is an endless and ever-expanding complex that we tap into. What good is this to those unwilling to listen?

We cannot force people to be good. We cannot force anything without breaking something else. Law is practice.

The law is simple, and obeyed by almost all creatures — give what you have to sustain those around you. The river lives not for the water, but for the fish. The tree lives for the birds, and the soil for the plants. The deer willingly gives himself to the wolf pack, if not driven by an inner consciousness, certainly driven by a greater consciousness. Live by giving. Take what you need; just make sure you pay for it.

The entire society of entitlement we see comes from the idea that there are those above the law. The lawbreaker is the lawgiver — he who presumes authority over his relatives. Corruption of the natural order is the basis of the ethos of domination. The rules are the same for all of us, for indeed we are all the same.

We should not have to state the obvious, but here we are. Turn towards home. State the obvious again and again, so that we may no longer be ruled by lies.

Truth is sacred. The only objective reality is our shared experience. Hold it close. Honor it. But use it. Remember that we win in the end. We survive and create peace in this world. It gets better. We get better. We ascend. Do not despair.

Epilogue

The speed at which we move is crucial. We may be spinning on a wheel too fast to think. Climate change? Impending doom? We're all going to die? The Zen "so what?" response is even more terrifying than the looming danger.

"Humans are a virus anyway" as Agent Smith used to say. And you believed him. "What does the Earth care if we all die? Or the Sun?" is the new cry of "reason" giving a green light to the ongoing destruction, paced at the same speed as the panic-stricken, savior-complex society.

Stop putting it out there. Know and generate more knowledge of our rise to liberation. Exalt our impending ascension. Murder and exploitation will become extinct — not us.

Spread utopia in thought, word and deed. We need it.

Turn Left

Take them with you.

Lead them into the Maze.

Guide them towards the Center.

Stalk the jungle.

Weave your web.

The Maze of Creation

Give birth to your light.

Remember that God is infinite.

Remember to remember.

The totality of the universe is divine.

So are all things within:

You, and everyone else,

All struggling to be loved.

Everything in this world is divine.

Life is the divine light.

Light is creation.

Creation is knowledge.

Knowledge is divine.

Divinity is infinite.

Epilogue

Within the whole — both the good and the bad are God.

We may rest in darkness, but must not deny the light.

Accept evil and suffering as crucial to the whole.

Faith is to know that light maintains a margin over darkness. This is the Center of the Maze. This is your heart within you — a channel to source. This is the source of love within you — a gate to forgiveness.

Regardless of what happens, light has the edge. Find it. Feed it. Cultivate truth with forgiveness and love. This is divine work. You are not only worthy, but mandated to act with the best of intentions.

Trust yourself.

Know the totality.

Know the infinite.

Know the divine.

Know yourself.

Be.

The Maze of Creation

Orphaned by conscience

Independent of inner conflict

Towards good or evil

You are now merely a node of refraction

For the dynamics of shine and shade

No longer a piece in the game

But part of the board

The Maze of Creation

You can have whatever you want in this world.

Just write it on the wall.

The consequences will be yours.

Holding on is everything...

The Maze of Creation

Until you let go.

Ricardo Tane Ward Ramirez

—2019—

The Maze of Creation

Biographical Details

Ricardo Tane Ward Ramirez is a scholar, writer and organizer based out of Austin, Texas. He writes poetry, nonfiction and fiction based on his experiences working in indigenous communities throughout North and South America most prominently with the Iku in Northern Colombia and the cultures of Tlaxcala, Mexico from where he descends. He earned his PhD in Anthropology in 2014 from the University of Texas.